THE CAPE WRATH TRAIL

DAVID PATERSON
PUBLISHED BY PEAK PUBLISHING

D1205453

First published in Great Britain by:
Peak Publishing Ltd.,
88 Cavendish Road,
London SW12 0DF.

ISBN 0 9521908 1 8

British Library cataloguing in Publication Data applied for.

Paterson, David
The Cape Wrath Trail
1. The Scottish Highlands
2. Long-distance walking
3. Photography

Designed by Peak Publishing
Typeset in Bookman 12/18
Originated and printed by Toppan Co (Singapore) Pte.

Contents

The Caledonian Canal at Banavie

*Ben Nevis from Corpach, the western
terminus of the Caledonian Canal*

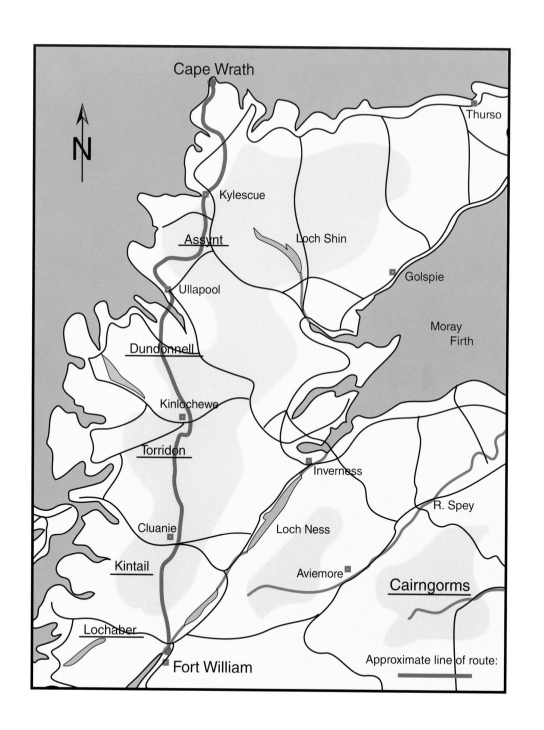

Cape Wrath

N

Thurso

Kylescue

Assynt

Loch Shin

Golspie

Ullapool

Moray
Firth

Dundonnell

Kinlochewe

Torridon

Inverness

R. Spey

Cluanie

Loch Ness

Kintail

Aviemore

Cairngorms

Lochaber

Fort William

Approximate line of route:

PREFACE

On the first of May, 1993, I set out from Fort William to walk, cross-country, two hundred and some miles through the north-west Highlands of Scotland, to Cape Wrath. The idea for this expedition had taken shape two years previously, as I worked on a book on The West Highland Way, which (for those who might not know) is a long-distance walking route from Glasgow to the Great Glen. Long before that book was complete, I had become deeply intrigued by the idea of trying to extend the route all the way to the north coast, to run the full length of the Highlands.

The existing trail finishes in Fort William; heading north from there, the only possible destination was that lonely northwest tip of the Scottish mainland which the Vikings had called *Wross* - The Turning Point. When *The West Highland Way* was at last complete, I settled down with maps to plan my walk.

I began by defining a set of rules which I hoped not to break too often. The line should run as closely as possible south to north; it should go through the best available scenery; it should try to shun paved roads, but follow existing footpaths whenever they were useful, and it should avoid crossing mountain ranges or major rivers except where absolutely necessary. It must be a route which walkers would feel able to tackle, and it should make sensible use of the occasional village, hotel or hostel for rest and resupply. I also wanted to visit the coast at least once in addition to the starting and finishing points.

A little map-work soon revealed a number of differences between my proposed route and the West Highland Way. It was, of course, more than twice as long, but the important differences were qualitative rather than quantitative. The West Highland Way climbs only one real mountain ridge, never crosses a river or stream except by a bridge, and follows fairly closely the main lines of communication through the south-central Highlands. It is a wonderful walk, but though the walking is all out in the open countryside, each night can be spent in comfortable lodgings, and little more needs to be carried than a waterproof, a change of socks and a toothbrush. The new route, on the other hand, would have to cross a two-thousand-foot ridge on only the second day, and another ridge and a fair-sized river the next. Obstacles might not always follow each other so frequently, but there would be more ridges and rivers to cross before the end, and opportunities for cozy nights in hotels or b&b would be limited. I thought the walk might take around eighteen days, and most of the nights would be spent in the wilds, putting up in bothies where possible, but sometimes in the open air.

I spent many an evening that winter poring over OS maps, tracing stalkers' paths and old drover's roads, measuring the distances and working out logistics, and just this was a lot of fun. The route I finally settled on begins at Banavie two miles to the east of Fort William, heads up the Great Glen to Loch Lochy, and turns north to cut across Glen Garry and Glen Shiel. It traverses the huge wilderness between Glen Sheil and Strathcarron, the mountains south and north of Glen Torridon, and the vastness of the Kinlochewe and Fisherfield deer-forests south of Dundonnell, to arrive in Ullapool by boat across Loch Broom. North of Ullapool, the route begins by following the coast, cuts through the Coigach and Assynt hills, then rolls for a day or two through the incomparable panorama of mountain, loch and moorland that is west Sutherland (Suilven, Canisp, Quinag, Ben More Assynt, Ben Stack, Arkle, Foinaven - what images those names conjure!).

Striking the west coast again at Rhiconich, the route now takes to the road through Kinlochbervie, and finishes with a windswept trek across the emptiness of Sandwood Bay and the lonely moorland south of Cape Wrath. My own arrival there, after completing the walk the first time, is a favourite memory.

In the three years which followed, I made many return visits to continue work on the photography, and the logistics of this were difficult, not least because the start of the route is nearly five hundred and fifty miles from my home. I always tried to leave on a good forecast, but this was rarely a guarantee of fine weather. On my first walk in May 1993, there was cloudy weather at the start, then rain; several days of great heat and thick haze; three days of driving snow; then rain, fog, and finally, at Cape Wrath itself, a day of sunshine and clear air. I managed very little useful photography that first time, and too many subsequent visits to the north-west suffered in much the same way.

Some parts of the route are remote from any road, and just reaching them and getting out again may commit the walker to two or more days on foot. As a result, there were a few sections which I simply never saw in fine weather, nor when visibility was good enough for photography. An example is the important piece of trail from Cluanie in Glen Shiel to the bothy at Ben Dronaig which I crossed three times, each time with an improving forecast, but each time in almost continuous rain. When I had finally to call time on my efforts to improve the collection of photographs, there were still more gaps in it than I liked.

On return visits to work on the pictures, I also wanted to clarify my ideas on certain parts of the route, as there were questions about the best alternatives at one or two points, especially in the last few days of the walk. Some of those questions are still very much open, and it would need other walkers to try the route and express their opinions, before a definitive line could emerge.

For those who might try the route, long-distance is very much the operative word, and like me, most walkers will, I think, find it a test of both endurance and sheer persistence. Among British walks, the Pennine Way, at two hundred and seventy-odd miles, is longer than this new route, but the nature of the terrain, the extreme remoteness of some of it, and the need for great self-reliance make the latter a harder proposition, in my opinion. I only walked it once - complete from end to end - and there were times during that walk when it seemed too much of a marathon, and part of me longed to give up. On later trips I would drive north and walk for just a few days along a couple of chosen sections.

The walk I have called The Cape Wrath Trail is one which measures up to the best in long-distance walks anywhere, and for scale and grandeur it will bear comparison with almost any Himalayan trek; I recommend it heartily. But there are no stocky, smiling porters, in Fort William or Ullapool, waiting to carry that aching rucksack!

David Paterson   October 1995

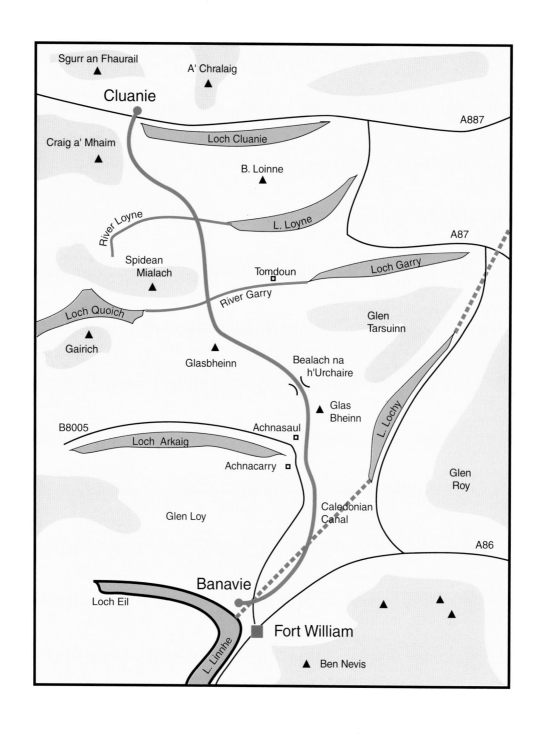

CHAPTER ONE
FORT WILLIAM TO GLEN SHIEL

1. Banavie to Bealach na h'Urchaire

Though in principle the route begins in Fort William, I allowed myself to miss out the first two miles of busy road, and set off from Banavie where road and rail cross the Caledonian Canal near its western terminus. Where the canal starts its long climb up the set of locks called Neptune's Staircase, I started out alone, early one soft May morning of cloud, light winds and patches of pale blue sky, along the broad tow-path on the south side of the water.

The prospect of this long foot-journey was enticing, not least because the idea of *journey* can hardly be separated (in my mind) from those of escape, adventure and exploration. Though there is little left in the world, let alone Scotland, which has not been mapped and measured, there still exists the possibility of personal exploration, in the sense of visiting and experiencing places new to oneself (if not to others), or testing oneself to new or different limits. I looked forward to the full measure of each during the following few weeks as I travelled the north-western Highlands from end to end, seeing many familiar landscapes afresh, and visiting lonely glens where the climbing trips of an entire lifetime might never take me.

Ben Nevis from Banavie

Starting out, I had little confidence that I could complete the walk at the first attempt. My pack weighed nearly forty pounds including camera equipment, and during previous experiences of long-distance walking, I had never carried nearly so much. This trip meant real back-packing, being totally self-sufficient for days at a time, and I thought my route might total a little over two hundred miles. If I couldn't make it all the way to Cape Wrath, I hoped at least to save face by getting as far as Kinlochewe, or perhaps Dundonnell just beyond half-way. But I knew to take things just one day at a time; the trick was to enjoy everything, to see everything, and to miss nothing important.

For half-a-mile at the start, yachts swayed at moorings along the canal. Beyond Banavie, both banks are tree-lined, and on that Mayday morning the trees were in the first burst of new leaf. Through them, and beyond the valley to the south, Ben Nevis and the Aonach hills were cloud-capped.

The canal towpath makes easy walking, flattering to the walker, and the first miles flow past. The views are all across the floor of the Great Glen: quiet pastoral scenes of grazing sheep and cattle, hay-fields, clumps of woodland. Along two stretches, at Strone and shortly before Gairlochy, the path runs narrowly between the canal on one hand and the river on the other, and beyond a spacious basin the canal merges with Loch Lochy.

Leaving the towpath, I swung left then right to take the single-track road past the western tip of the loch to Achnacarry, and on to Loch Arkaig. I had imagined my first night's bivouac (I wasn't carrying a tent) would be somewhere there in the woods which fringe the loch, but though my feet were a little sore I felt strong; the sky was clearing and there were hours of daylight left. In an excess of enthusiasm I rounded the end of Loch Arkaig, and where a stream crosses the road at Achnasaul, I turned uphill following a narrow path on the right bank of the water.

The path climbs steeply up alongside the stream, fringed with birch, rowan and pine, and where I first stepped into the trees, a red-deer hind, long dead, lay in a hollow beneath a fallen trunk where she had crept for shelter, or to die. She was the first of many I would see, casualties of a long winter of deep snow only recently melted from the hills, the carcasses not yet picked clean and scattered by scavenging foxes. Above the trees, the slope eased and the path broadened and continued up a narrow glen below the blunt cone of Glas Bheinn, covered with new grass and the very image of its name - Green Hill.

(Top) Autumn colours at Kilmonivaig

Caledonian Canal at Gairlochy

Loch Arkaig at sunset

From a lush meadow with meandering streams in a hollow behind the hill, my route continued north, now trackless for a spell, up to the pass called Bealach na h'Urchaire. As I gained height up heather slopes broken by peat-hags, the deep and distant recesses of Glen Tarsuinn opened below to the east, and yellow evening light spilled west along Loch Arkaig to the wilderness of Glen Dessary and Knoydart. Nearing the pass, I came suddenly on a single hind with her new calf, which both fled in moments over the ridge I was also making for - getting slow now and tired - at the end of what had been a very long day.

At the watershed, Ben Nevis, streaked with snow, dominated the southern horizon; north, the peaks of Glenquoich and Glen Sheil rose from shadow where the forests of Glen Garry had already lost the sun. The wind had dropped and an absolute calm spread over the landscape as colours deepened towards twilight; far down in the northern valley a single light snapped on as darkness fell. Tired, but too full of pure exultation to settle down for the night, I sat and gazed out over the silent hills until it became too dark to see. Finally, laying my sleeping-bag down on a soft bank of moss and heather, I slept by the tiny lochan at the col, in the wind-shelter of a rocky mound.

2. Bealach na h-Urchaire to Glen Garry.

In the very early morning I woke, cold, to find rime on my sleeping bag and ice in my beard and moustache; there was a bright full moon and stars overhead, and a sharp frost. I lay, vainly trying to sleep in spite of the fierce cold, until at around five-fifteen am the sun burst over the horizon and warmed me within minutes, so that I slept soundly for almost another three hours.

Up at two thousand feet, it was still winter. As I made my breakfast coffee, there was a skein of ice on the lochan, and the hills above the col had patches of old snow I hadn't noticed in the semi-dark of the previous night. Underfoot, the sparse vegetation had the faded, grey-brown look of being too long covered by snow, and there was no sign here of new growth. Stiff after my long first day's walk - 15 miles or more - I hobbled off down the northern slopes of the bealach to try to pick up the next stalkers' path, heading for Glen Garry by the waters of the Allt Ailein.

Glas Bheinn and the Nevis range,
from Bealach na h'Urchaire

The River Garry and Ben Gairich

(Top) Keeper's howf on the Allt Ailein
above Glen Garry

The forest floor,
Glen Garry

Deer below Spidean Mialach, in Glen Garry

More hard drifts of old snow lay in sheltered hollows far down these slopes, and small groups of red-deer hinds and calves watched nervously as I picked my way downhill, while brief glimmers of sunshine alternated with squalls of cold north wind. The path was quickly found, and I followed it all morning down to a muddy gateway at the upper edge of a conifer plantation above the River Garry. The gate in the deer-fence was broken, and hundreds of hoof-prints leading into the wood showed that the deer were not slow to take advantage. Nearby trees were stripped of all reachable bark, their bared trunks gleaming nakedly among the dark foliage.

Under the trees, the path led easily down pleasant slopes and through warm sheltered clearings to cross the Allt Choire Bhalachain, an energetic stream tumbling downhill in a succession of rapids, short waterfalls and glissades over stepped pavements of smooth rock. Beyond the burn, the remains of an old forestry hut were being slowly crushed between vigourous young conifers. Again, I had imagined my night's rest being among these fragrant firs and spruces, perhaps within earshot of the River Garry, but it was too early in the day to stop. I followed a good forestry track to the bridge below Aultnaslat and turned east to head for the Tomdoun Inn and an unplanned night of comfort and good food. The hotel (and its bothy - £1.00 per night) was just two miles away, and had long been a favourite. Including this extra stretch, the day's walk had been an easy seven miles.

3. Glen Garry to Cluanie.

In the morning I hitched back along the road to Aultnaslat, and picking up my route again, walked two miles west along the road to a stone bridge beside a small grove of birches and alders. Here, a stalkers' path leads up the right bank of the stream to an unnamed col below the ridge of Spidean Mialach, (the peak just east of Gleouraich - the wonderfully named Hill of Roaring). The morning was fine, with the same mix of sun and showers, and a cool northerly breeze. A good path climbed steadily a thousand feet to the col which opened like a door, quite suddenly, into the echoing vastness of upper Glen Loyne, a valley of almost Himalayan proportions, so that the mind struggles with the enormity of the glacier which must once have carved it.

To the north, Creag a' Mhaim and the peaks of the Cluanie Forest were snow-streaked under lowering cloud. A good path leads on into Glen Loyne from the col, passing a pair of large Scots pines on the descent, and as I admired these examples of my favourite trees, a peregrine rose from the nearer of the two with its typical high scream, and soared off across the glen. The stalker's track swung round, heading west up Glen Loyne before descending to the river, and making much too long a detour for my liking. I turned north, following the flight of the peregrine, past a group of dead pines which raised gaunt branches against a sky turned blue again, and splashed across the broad, gravelly shallows of the River Loyne.

The previous day, the River Garry had been high when I crossed the bridge at Aultnaslat, and I wondered about this crossing of the Loyne. But Highland rivers don't stay long in spate since the hills are built of rock with only the thinnest covering of soil, and drain rapidly. On this occasion I was lucky; on a later visit, I did meet a disconsolate group of walkers at the Tomdoun Inn, who had just been turned back by the Loyne in full flood.

Already, on only the third day of the walk, the terrible emptiness of these glens was impossible to ignore. Glen Loyne may never have been inhabited during historic times, and there are no obvious traces of past occupation - no crumbling walls or roofless crofts, nor any blurred outlines of ancient fields. In general, however, the region was well-populated until the spectre of the Clearances raised its head in the late 18th century, and the tragedy of Glen Garry and its people was the prototype for everything that was to happen throughout the Highlands. In cycles lasting seventy years, the glens were cleared of their people to permit large-scale sheep-farming, but even this was insufficient to halt the descent into debt of the absurd MacDonnell chiefs, and at last the land itself had to be parcelled up and sold off. When it was over, hardly a Macdonnell was left on clan lands which had stretched thirty miles from the Great Glen to the coast of Morar. Betrayed and abandoned, the MacDonnells were forced into emigration and scattered through the wilds of Canada; so thoroughly were their home glens depopulated that they have remained virtually empty to this day.

Having taken a short-cut down to the river, I was now off my intended path, but knew that by circling east below the cliffs of Creag Liathtais, the south-east spur of Creag a'Mhaim, I would soon come on the stream called Allt Giubhais. Following this steeply up past rapids and waterfalls, and getting hot in the process, I was surprised by a sudden snow-shower falling from clouds which had gathered again, and were dark overhead. The squall lasted fifteen minutes, and when it stopped I struck uphill again, and soon came on the old road (originally built by Thomas Telford) from Tomdoun to Cluanie, closed to traffic, but perhaps still passable on foot after a spell of dry weather. The road crossed Loch Loyne on a causeway, but since a hydro-electric scheme raised the level of the loch it can only be passed now when the water is low. More recently, one of the local estates is rumoured to have dynamited the causeway.

Once on the old road, navigation was easy, and the remainder of the day's walk was a mere stroll down through fine scenery to the Cluanie Inn, nestling below the green hills of Glen Shiel. In recent times Glen Shiel has become a major tourist draw. The scenery is superb; long ridges descend on both sides of the valley from distant, often shapely, summits; there are eleven Munros along the north flank, and an almost equal number to the south. On Loch Duich, at the west end of the Glen, Eilan Donan Castle stands on an island at the end of a causeway, and though the present building is a twentieth-century reconstruction, the site has an interesting history, and fortifications have stood there since the early 13th century, when they were first built for protection against the Vikings. In 1719 it was the scene of the last real battle in the western Highlands, when a Jacobite adventure was put down by Government forces which bombarded the castle from frigates, reducing most of it to rubble.

The day's effort had been ten and a half miles in a little over five hours. Cluanie was the first of several landmarks which I had set for myself in the course of the walk, and I knew that it was important to have reached it in good form. Now I could permit myself to think ahead somewhat, and to believe that I would at least reach my next milestone at Strathcarron, three days' walk away across the biggest wilderness in the West Highlands.

Glen Loyne and Creag a' Mhaim

The Cluanie Inn and Sgurr an Fhuarail

Glen Shiel near the Cluanie Inn

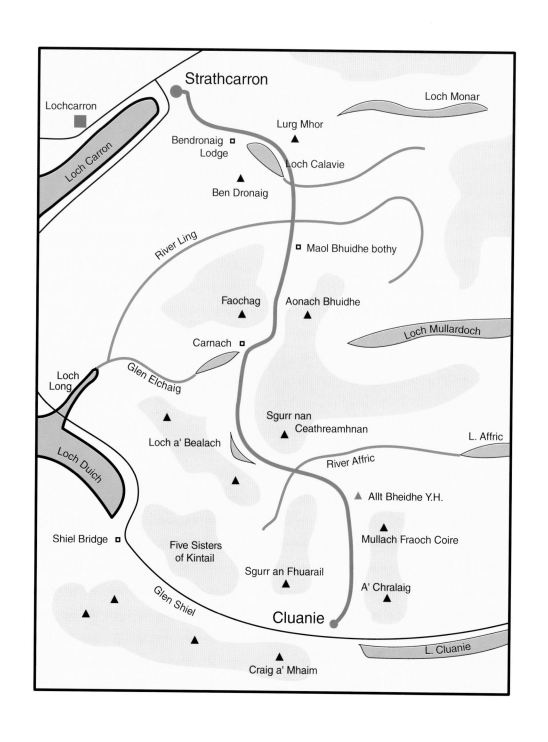

CHAPTER TWO
GLEN SHIEL TO STRATHCARRON

1. Cluanie to Carnach.

The next morning there was too much cloud about for comfort, but it was boiling, shifting, and at times there were fleeting patches of blue. I set off along the main road, heading east a mile to the southern end of An Caorann Mor, a tremendous glacial valley which would take me north, to the headwaters of the River Affric, and the great wilderness I hoped to cross in the next three days. Hemmed in between high mountain walls whose ridges barely fall below three thousand feet, An Caorann Mor is less a valley than a trench, whose dramatic over-steepened side-walls lead the eye up to dark and distant summits. It was easy to feel overwhelmed by the scale of the surroundings as the path disappeared into the distance

Craig a'Mhaim, above Cluanie

below brooding slopes, and cloud drifted around the tops, adding to their mystery.

The path was excellent at first, but after a couple of miles deteriorated to become no more than a wet scar along the weeping lower slopes of Mullach Fraoch Choire ('The Summit of the Heather Corrie'). It was leading to the youth hostel at Alltbheithe, the most remote in Scotland, situated at the half-way point of the long right-of-way which leads from lower Glen Affric through to Loch Duich. Below Mullach Fraoch Choire, maps show a path descending to the River Affric, and though I somehow missed this, I dropped down to the river anyway and crossed it easily, wading the shallows and leaping a final deeper channel.

Looking across An Caorann Mor to A' Chralaig

On the far bank a path led west into Gleann Gniomhaidh and under the northern corries of Beinn Fhada. Far behind, patches of blue sky and dappled light on the hills east of Alltbheidhe made it seem as if the weather might improve, but ahead the sky was darker and the clouds lower. At the head of the glen, where it turns to the north and becomes Glen Gorsaic, I crossed a barely perceptible water-shed and began a gentle descent towards the chain of lochans which lie cupped between Beinn Fhada and Sgurr nan Ceathreamhnan.

The scene could scarcely have been more dramatic. Tall black cliffs and beetling slopes rose into swirling masses of dark cloud and descended to the shores of Loch a Bhealaich which lay, sullen and uninviting, in its peaty hollow. The landscape was harsh, torn by apparently cataclysmic events, unsoftened by even a single tree or bush. The path had disappeared at the watershed; I didn't expect to pick up the next until well down Glen Gorsaic, and underfoot the going was rough and wet. In the morning, I had earmarked this corner of the hills as a possible stopping-place for the night, ten miles from the morning's start at Cluanie, but there was nothing which offered the least possibility of shelter, and now I carried on without the need for any conscious decision.

The River Gorsaic begins life in the string of lochans of which Loch a Bhealaich, with its solitary tree-clad island, is the largest. The others wander down the glen in a boggy flatland which grows greener the further it emerges from the surrounding cliffs, until the last ponds and meanders are reed-lined and decked with lilies. I kept well up the hillside, out of the bogs and peat-hags, until some distance beyond the last loch in the chain I spotted a couple of cairns. It seemed likely that these were landmarks of some kind - a visual aid in poor weather - and it came as no surprise when a good, dry path appeared.

Scotland's most famous waterfall - the Falls of Glomach - was just a mile or so off to my left, but in such poor weather, with thirteen miles already under my belt that day and an unknown distance still to go to find shelter, I wasn't tempted to make the detour. There was obviously going to be a lot of rain again quite soon, and with the primitive bivouac gear I was carrying (a large plastic bag!) the desire to find cover for the night was strong.

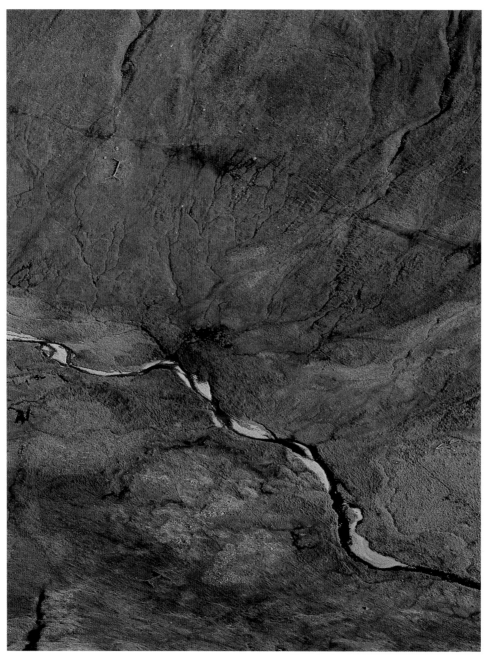

The Allt Bheithe track

(Top) Loch a' Bealach, Glen Gniomhaidh

Looking north, Glen Gorsaic

At the end of Loch Lon Mhurchaidh the path suddenly plunged down the side of a gorge via a precipitous grassy ridge. On the left a tall waterfall hissed down in a corner of the crags, and some hundreds of feet lower, the ravine opened out and the stream merged with a larger river. On its far banks were pastures, cowsheds, and a couple of neat houses, a dirt road and a line of telegraph poles. Although I knew from the map that this was Carnach, I hadn't anticipated so much, so far from any public road - a couple of tumbledown bothies, perhaps, but not a major conurbation!

Even from a distance, however, it was soon obvious that the cottages were shuttered, that no smoke rose from any of the chimneys, and that Carnach was unoccupied, if not exactly abandoned. Darkness was approaching, and I hurried to make some arrangement for the night. The best bet seemed to be a small cowshed, open along one side - there was rain already on the wind, but as long as it came from the north I would be sheltered. In the shed there was some clearing of dried cow-dung to be done, but a shovel stood handily in a corner, and once its covering had been removed, the cement floor was dry and almost clean. I laid out my sleeping-bag to avoid the worst of the drips from the roof; stove purring companionably and candle trying to keep the gathering darkness at bay, I began to make myself comfortable for the night. Later, heavy rain came hammering on the roof and woke me in the small hours several times, but the wind never shifted from the north and I stayed warm and dry till morning.

2. Carnach to Bendronaig Lodge.

There was very little improvement in the next morning's weather, and no choice but to set off in a steady drizzle. Carnach lies in Glen Elchaig, and for a mile my route followed the unpaved road north-east up the valley. At Iron Lodge, where a corrugated-iron shooting lodge must once stood, I took the glen which heads north between the peaks of Faochaig and Aonach Buidhe. No tops were visible however, on this dismal morning, and the crags of Faochaig disappeared into a blanket of grey, weeping cloud. The path, clearly marked, climbed steadily up the glen which opened out and levelled to become a broad strath with wide prospects all round. For the second day in a row, these hills and glens

Bog pine near Maol-bhuidhe

were alive with deer, and large groups of both hinds and stags stood, tails to the weather, watching calmly as I tramped past.

The rest of the track to the Maol-bhuidhe bothy lay across an almost level moorland and I bitterly regretted the poor weather and longed for sun and open skies to enjoy these new landscapes, now hidden in clouds and mist. At the bothy there was no sign of life. The exterior was neat, trim and weatherproof, and much of the interior was in good repair, if rather lacking furnishings; sadly, the ready presence of a bushman saw and large axe had encouraged previous visitors to hack down, for the fire, some of the pine lining inside the cottage. (There can be no excuse for this kind of behaviour, and the people who do it may still regard themselves as mountaineers or walkers, but in fact are mere vandals.)

During my brief stay the sky lightened a little, and the clouds lifted enough to reveal Ben Dronaig filling the horizon close by to the north and west. From Maol Bhuidhe a trail leads away east towards Loch Monar, but my route lay north across the River Ling and round the end of Ben Dronaig. This remote river-crossing was another I had worried over, and there were warnings posted prominently in the bothy. In the event, however, the water was very low and I splashed across, with just one long stride over a deeper channel under the far bank. Flotsam on both banks of the stream, however, marked how high the Ling could rise after prolonged rain, and it would be a dangerous proposition in full spate.

Onwards there was no discernable track for more than a mile, but the map showed a stalker's path spiralling down the east ridge of Ben Dronaig, and by walking a rising traverse round the hill I was bound to cross it. Soon there were white-washed rocks visible every fifty yards or so, and with them the path which in minutes led me to Loch Calavie, cradled between Ben Dronaig and Lurg Mhor. At the end of the loch, beaches of orange sand and a rope bridge across a stream enlivened the scene as a weak and watery sun made a brief appearance; on the north shore, the best path I had walked so far clung to the very edge of the loch, where wavelets slapped the stones, and took me west towards Ben Dronaig Lodge, still two or three miles away.

I had no idea what there might be there - perhaps nothing, as at Iron Lodge that morning, but after a mile the path shot from between the narrow jaws of Coire na Sorna, and broad views opened out towards the rolling hills of Attadale. There was a good bridge across a stream; in the distance by a grove of birch trees stood a shooting lodge clad in corrugated iron, and beside it, a fine little bothy. I called out as I approached, but both buildings were deserted. In a shaky lean-to at the end of the cottage wood was stacked, and in the slightly musty interior a couple of old chairs, a rickety bed, a fireplace, a bottle with a stub of candle, and an old copy of 'Kidnapped' was the complete inventory. But what luxury, what excess, after the night before. I gleaned fallen wood from beneath the trees, leaving the stacked timber to the rightful owners or those in greater need, and in the hearth built a fire to last the evening.

3. Ben Dronaig to Strathcarron.

In the morning I lay for what seemed a long time, peering from my bedroll in front of the hearth through the murky glass of the window, trying to make up my mind whether the sky was grey or blue. Realising it was blue, I shot out of bed and rubbed clear the corner of a dusty pane. Outside, the still-early sun cast long shadows under the birches where red-deer hinds and calves grazed innocently; in the distance, mist streamed from a circle of hazy summits. There was no great hurry to be away - there was all day, if necessary, to reach Strathcarron only six and a half miles away. I dawdled for an hour in the grassy meadows around the lodge, luxuriating in the glorious solitude of the place, before hoisting my pack and setting out at mid-morning.

A good dirt road leads all the way from the lodge to Attadale on Loch Carron-side, and I followed it for a mile or so, across the rocky gorge of the Black Water, until it began to trend a little south where I wanted to trend a little north. With no sign of a footpath, I headed for a rusty fence on the skyline half a mile off, which went in my desired direction; underfoot the terrain was unpleasant for a mile or so, all loose gravel, and stones which rolled beneath the feet. There was a fine view down the birch-filled gully of Eas Ban - White Water - and from the highest point of the track, a glimpse of a distant peak - a white cone, misty and ethereal, floating above the ground-haze like Mt Fuji in a Japanese print.

The bothy at Ben Dronaig Lodge

This apparition was Spidean a' Choire Leith, the summit of Liathach in Torridon, seen through the narrow cleft of Bealach Ban in the mountains of north of Strathcarron. (My route would take me through there the next day to a bivouac below Liathach itself).

There were no more such magical visions, but a pretty lochan or two as the path rolled on, easily now, through undulating heather country. Soon the houses of Achintee were spread below me, and beyond them Strathcarron, a green oasis in a wilderness of brown hills. To the west, the sun glinted sharply on Loch Carron - my first sight of the sea since leaving Loch Linnhe at Fort William.

The Dingwall to Kyle of Lochalsh railway (famous all around the world among train enthusiasts for its unique Highland scenery) comes through this glen, and I followed a tarmac road down past the small group of houses at Achintee and round to the little hotel by Strathcarron station, to the end of another days' walk. My tally of miles had now reached beyond sixty, and though my daily average of only ten miles was less than I had hoped for, I was beginning to entertain thoughts of reaching Cape Wrath, after all.

Loch an Fheoir, on the Ben Dronaig path

Frosted birches in the Eas Ban gully

Achintee and Strathcarron

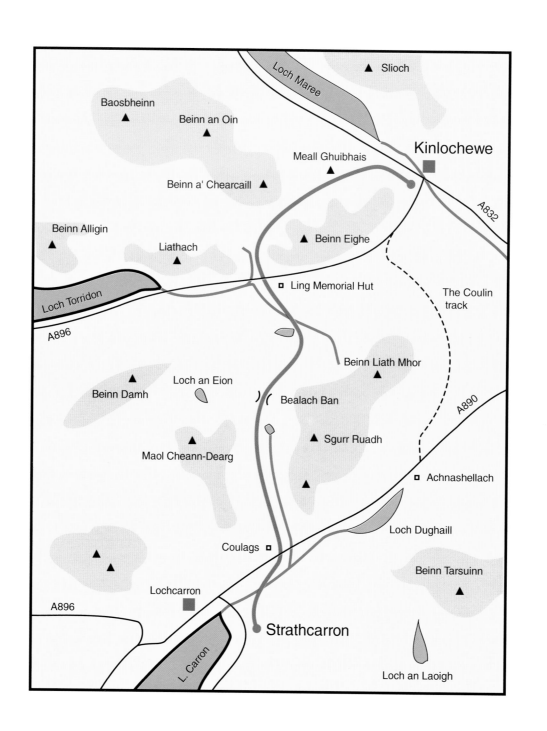

CHAPTER THREE
STRATHCARRON TO KINLOCHEWE

1. Strathcarron to Glen Torridon

From the station, my route follows the main road north for half a mile, over the river, to a farm track on the right. (The farm is called New Kelso, and must surely have an exile from the borders somewhere in its history.) Beyond a row of cottages and a good steading, the track leads across fields to the north bank of the River Carron which was wide, smooth and fast-flowing, and with my fear of river-crossings, I was glad to have been able to cross it by a bridge. At the junction of the Carron

Strathcarron

and a northern tributary, a large, wooded island hides the actual point of confluence, and on the left a spruce plantation screens the nearby Lochcarron road. When the track wandered off into the trees, I stuck to the bank of the river that was now the Fionn Abhainn (Bright Water), which after another few hundred yards began to swing towards the north. Where the main road crosses the stream, a footpath heading due north into the hills could be seen just by the cottages at Coulags.

The day was really fine and hot, though the haze that was to trouble me, photographically, for the next few days was already thickening. The right-of-way which I was following (one of several crossing the hill-passes of the Ben Damph and Coulin Forests) climbed steadily up beside the stream as the mountain ridges on either side grew in height. Some way up the corrie, a single rowan-tree stood by a trim bothy not marked on the map, and I regretted not knowing of its existence, since an easy walk up here the previous evening would have put me in the heart of the mountains for sun-up. A little further along the trail, The Rock of the White Dogs (Clach nan Con-fionn) sat on its haunches near the trail, looking from some angles uncannily like a dog, and in the legends of Fingal the Hunter, was the rock to which he tethered his deer-hounds.

At the head of the corrie, a sizeable lochan shimmered in the heat below the screes of Sgorr Ruadh, and the path kept closely along its western shore before beginning a steep climb up to the pass into Glen Torridon. This was Bealach Ban, the gap through which I had glimpsed the summit of Liathach the previous day. Where the trail forks, I took the left branch to detour for half-an-hour and look at the parallel pass of Bealach na Lice, which leads down into Glen Torridon by a more westerly route. Its situation is superb; the summit of Maol Chean-dearg looms directly above, and Beinn na h'Eaglaise and Beinn Damh rise immediately beyond a group of small lochs, of which the biggest, Loch an Eoin, is set beautifully with islands. Cliffs, crags and slabs of rock surround the floor of

the glen which is strewn with massive blocks of Torridonian sandstone. The drama of this scene, with its sharp profiles and vertical exposures of rock, was in great contrast to the quieter landscapes of the two previous days of broad straths and gentle contours.

I retraced my steps towards Bealach Ban, meeting two fell-runners - my first humans since south of Cluanie - and made the final climb up to the pass. Across the deep rift of Glen Torridon, the haze softened, but could not hide, the massive walls of Liathach and Beinn Eighe which dominated the northern horizon. The perfect summit cone of Liathach was cloud-capped, and the sumptuous ridge of Beinn Eighe soared from top to top, a covering of white quartzite glinting like snow in the afternoon sun. Down in Glen Torridon, at least three miles away and fifteen hundred feet below, coloured dots crept along a black pencil-line which was the road, and a gleam of white beside the River Torridon was the Ling Memorial Hut, a climbing-base.

From the pass, the path contours for a few hundred yards over rocky slopes below Sgurr Ban then turns abruptly downhill in one long swoop towards the climbing hut and the river.

Loch Fionn Choire, below Bealach Ban

Sgurr Ban from Bealach Ban

I started down as the sun, lowering in the west, began to pick out with shadow a sea of drumlins - ancient mounds of glacial debris - on the valley-floor. At once a plump hare darted out from beneath my feet; I was certainly the more startled of the two.

Downhill is always easy; I covered the three miles to the river in an hour on an excellent path, stopping only to chat for a few minutes with some climbers at the Ling hut. I knew I wouldn't be spending the night there - it is nearly always full in the summer months, and in any case, bed-space must be booked in advance through a club - my night's stop lay a little further on. Beyond the road, the walls and gable of a ruined croft-house stand in grassy meadows beside the stream called the Allt Choire Dubh, which drains the high valley between Liathach and Beinn Eighe.

I tucked my heavy pack behind the tumbled walls and climbed a few hundred feet up the lower slopes of Liathach, to lie in the new bracken and watch the evening shadows begin their slow ascent of the massive sandstone walls of the south Torridon peaks. At eight pm hunger drove me back down to prepare a meal and later make a bed on soft turf in the lee of the ruins. Overhead, the evening sky was almost cloudless and there seemed little chance of rain; in the darkest part of the night I woke briefly, to see the surrounding ridges outlined against bright stars in a sky of, literally, midnight blue.

2. Glen Torridon to Kinlochewe.

In the east-west valley, the sun was with me early and I didn't lie long, once awake. The onward path was familiar for the first time since leaving the Caledonian Canal, and I had walked up Coire Dubh two or three times previously, to the stunning northern coire of Beinn Eighe and its famous triple buttress. There is drama all along this section of trail as it sweeps north and west under the cliffs of Liathach and Carn na Feola, and through the gap between them and the steep screes of Beinn Eighe. As height is gained, views to the north begin to open out, and where the path turns to begin its long spiralling ascent into the mouth of Coire Mhic Fhearchair, a superb western panorama also emerges. This is a wild, primitive landscape, from this distance seemingly quite untouched by man, and the uncompromising shapes of Beinn an Eoin,

Bhaosbheinn and Beinn a'Chearcaill erupt from the treeless glens - powerful, evocative, and supremely memorable.

I climbed all the way up to the sandstone plateau which rims the corrie, and stepped across a clear, crystal stream issuing from the loch, which glinted from its basin below the deeply-shaded cliffs of the celebrated triple buttress. Across from this high platform, Beinn a' Chearcaill was flanked on either side by glens running north, but my continuation eastwards was hidden behind the huge bulk of the northern summit of Beinn Eighe, and I contoured below it, threading down through small crags but maintaining as much height as possible. Once past the lowest rocks of Ruadh Stac Mhor, I descended to the valley floor, which sparkled everywhere with water, and began a long turn east towards unseen Kinlochewe. For a mile or more, as I crossed the glen, there was no trail to follow and I took my bearings deliberately, as there is the possibility here of heading north up Glen Grudie, which lies straight ahead - a tempting prospect to the careless map-reader. When this error had been avoided, the correct way was obvious: on the right, the towering ridges

Beinn an Eoin (left), and Beinn a'Chearcaill

and deep corries of Beinn Eighe's north face, and on the left, across a sizeable stream, the smooth green cone of Meall a' Ghuibhais. Between them, easy ground led eastwards.

The Beinn Eighe footpath

The Beinn Eighe ridge

*Looking west between Beinn Eighe (left)
and Meall a Ghuibhais*

Heather slopes rose slowly to an undulating skyline some two miles away. Avoiding the worst of some boggy stretches, and fording several streams, I headed that way, and by keeping over towards the north side of the glen soon struck the anticipated path. This was sketchy at first, and making my way uphill, I was rarely sure whether I was on a path or just a deer-trail, in spite of what the map was telling me. When I finally reached the skyline, this turned out to be the water-shed (marked by two tiny lochans) whose northern slopes drain into Loch Maree.

Beinn Eighe is a National Nature Reserve, and earlier I had seen something which was probably a Nature Reserve construction - just off my route a shape had appeared among the rocks that seemed not entirely natural. This turned out to be a well-camouflaged refuge or hide: cement-floored, iron-roofed and turf-covered, its spartan interior equipped with bench, stove, gas and candles. Only the door, which was hanging off its hinges, spoiled the *tout ensemble.* I took a quick look, made a cup of tea and left, wedging the door tightly shut. (On a trip the following winter, I failed to find it, drifted over in deep February snow.)

Across the valley beyond Kinlochewe, low hills were gold in the late afternoon sunshine as I strolled down a rapidly improving trail with strong wooden bridges over the larger streams. The haze allowed no more than a vague impression of anything more distant, but down in the valley itself, green fields were surrounded by the dark shadow of pine-woods. The path descended open slopes, and at the entrance to a belt of conifers it crossed a minor stream; just below was the A832 and I turned right on to the road, to walk another mile into Kinlochewe, the first proper village since the start of the walk.

It was early, and after eight days' walking I was ready to take it easy for a few hours, to indulge in the relative novelties of shopping, phoning home, having a beer or two, and later stretching out in a hot bath. I had covered about eighty-five miles in the eight days, and though this was still a little slower than I might have hoped, the halfway point was in my sights and I knew that my pace would soon accelerate with increasing fitness. The weather forecast was stable, and some of the most exciting country was still to come; in my head I was already celebrating at Cape Wrath.

Icicles on the stream below Coire Mhic Fhearchair

(Top) Slioch & Beinn a Mhuinidh, in cloud

The Kinlochewe valley

Frosted rowan, Kinlochewe

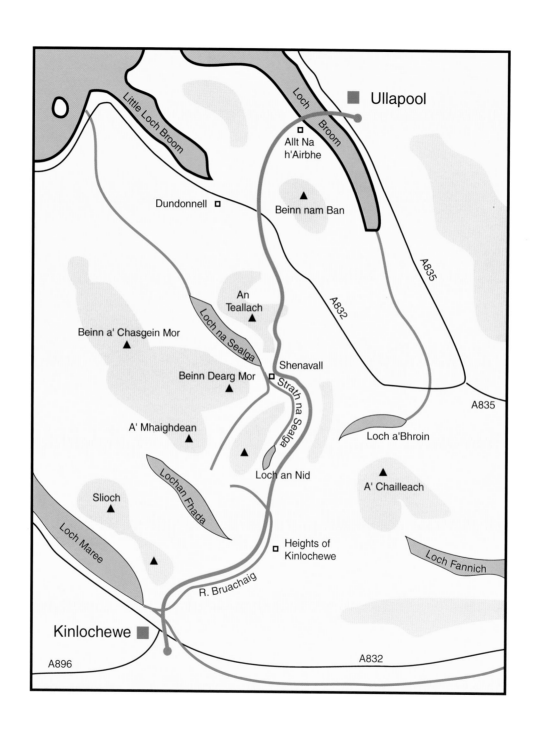

Chapter Four
Kinlochewe to Ullapool

1. Kinlochewe to Shenavall

Another day dawned fine, and I was up and away in good time. From Kinlochewe my route takes the main road east for half a mile, then the minor road to Incheril, past a cross-roads and school to a large new car-park. The latter wasn't there when I first walked the route. Then, the lane out of the village led to a padlocked gate topped by a ferocious message to all walkers and climbers, warning them off from August until February. I had heard that the Kinlochewe and Fisherfield estates, through which I was about to pass, had a reputation among walkers for being 'anti' and confrontational, but I didn't know if this was accurate, and had no first-hand knowledge. In the event, I simply climbed the stile and

The Glen Bruachaig track

carried quietly on my way, without incident. That was in 1993. Since then there has been a sea-change, and not only has the new car-park been built on estate land, but the draconian notice has gone, and now there is a warning of restrictions which apply only during the stalking season, and advice about dangers in the hills. It is wonderful to see a major estate adopt such a progressive stance; perhaps others will follow; it will be up to walkers and climbers to respond in like spirit.

Beyond Incheril, I took the good Landrover track towards the hill-farm at the Heights of Kinlochewe. The walking is easy, and the track follows the left bank of the River Bruachaig through sparse birch-groves and past waterfalls tumbing down high crags on the far side of the river. Near the farm, a cottage on the right of the track is in use as a bothy, and has the usual lack of all amenities except a hearth, and a roof and walls to keep the weather out - but who needs more? I looked briefly through the door, but it was too early in the day to be thinking of bothies, and where the track divides I took the left fork which climbs towards Gleann na Muice, and plodded on, in growing heat. Halfway up, a buzzard floated slowly overhead.

At the head of the glen the terrific panorama around Lochan Fhada opened out: Slioch to the south-west, Ben Lair, A'Mhaighdean, Mullach Coire Mhic Fhearchair and Sgurr Dubh, and to the east a sea of rolling hills disappearing off into the haze. I turned away from the loch, taking a path which climbed a short distance to a long-abandoned sheiling. Above it, easy heather slopes rose to an un-named bealach dotted with sedgy lochans, beyond which a route could be threaded down through deep peat-hags to a charming grassy hollow with a sparkling stream, where I lolled a while and ate some lunch. The next pass, Bealach na Crois, was directly above,

and looked formidable - a narrow gash below the crags of Sgurr Dubh - but in fact was only a stroll up then down pleasant grassy slopes beside another tinkling stream. Just over the top a path appeared, not marked on my map but heading the right way, and I followed it down into the long, lovely glen which holds Loch an Nid. Prodigious peaks, slabs and ridges soon appeared along the west side of the valley, with a great hogsback to the east, and An Teallach lying massively along the northern horizon, six or seven miles away.

At the loch I left the path to follow the west bank and investigate a series of enormous glacial slabs low down on the slopes of Sgurr Bhan. They proved impossible to photograph without another human form to give them scale, but fascinating to explore and scramble on, until round the northern end of the loch I regained the path where a waterfall cascades, in several tiers, down giant limestone steps into a black and sunless pool.

Further on, there were signs of habitation in this valley - field-clearance cairns and the softened outlines of ancient enclosures - and at the place named Achnelgie, where I entered Strath na Sealga, some low, scattered ruins.

Rocks along the River Bruachaig

The Heights of Kinlochewe

Slioch and Lochan Fada

(Opp) Loch Meallan an Fhudair, and
Mullach Coire Mhic Fhearchair

Winter, above Lochan Fada

There was ample firewood and water nearby, and I thought of making a bivouac here in the lee of the ruined walls of Achnelgie, as I had two days before in Glen Torridon, but the place had a sad atmosphere, and imaginings of people and families perhaps once happy here, now long gone, kept intruding.

I was tired and had already walked further than on any previous day, but the bothy at Shenavall was only a long mile further, and drew me on. En route a magical grove of alders held me in thrall for a while, and I put down my pack to explore more easily. Under the trees, the evening air was warm and still, with a resiny fragrance. Only the murmuring of the Strath na Sealga river broke a palpable silence, the topmost leaves shivered delicately in a phantom breeze, and red-deer cropped peacefully at new grass a few yards away across the river, untroubled by my presence, lifting their heads from time to time to hold me in an unblinking gaze. The sun was sinking in a blaze of yellow out beyond Loch na Sealga, and golden light streamed through the grove. Time stood still, and I wandered through the trees enraptured. It was that kind of moment when it is possible to think

you can detect, in the atmosphere of a quiet, solitary place, 'something more than the merely physical'. Before it became too dark to see, I shouldered my pack, and picking up dry timber for the fire as I walked, headed for Shenavall through the gloaming.

At the bothy I dropped my pack again and walked far enough to see the last remnants of sunset along Loch na Sealga, where Beinn Dearg Beg was silhouetted against a dark blue sky and faint streamers of pink cloud. The rest of the evening was unexceptional apart from my fire, which was especially good. Before I turned in, I looked around the bothy, which was large and had clearly once been comfortable, with hot water, baths and basins, flush toilets (which still worked if you got a bucket of water from the stream, a notice said), sprung beds and wooden armchairs. All this was still there, though hardly in prime condition, but I was glad that rumours of vandalism at Shenavall turned out to be untrue, or greatly exaggerated.

I've been back several times since then, to Shenavall, Achnelgie, and the grove of alders, and Strath na Sealga will aways be a very special place for me - the Strath of Hunting.

2. *Strath na Sealga to Ullapool.*

The morning was not as mystical as the evening had been, but Shenavall in the pre-dawn was still a beautiful place and I was sad to leave, even when the sun came up in a flood of hard light, bringing haze with it.

On a later visit I walked in to the bothy one evening from Dundonnell, and again was up before sunrise, to be in good position for the earliest, most beautiful light. As I picked my way in semi-darkness along the footpath heading west from the bothy, a huge stag - a ten-pointer - rose, grunting and steaming, from the heather just twenty yards ahead. This was the rutting season, and the previous winter, I had had a nervy encounter with an aggressive stag; this one took a step or two towards me as I backed off slowly; when he paused for a moment I raised both arms high and wide, and shouted at him. With a cough he swung away and trotted, stiff-legged, over to his hinds a hundred yards away, where he re-asserted his machismo by repeated loud roaring, while I withdrew, relieved.

Maps show a footpath (of which I could find no trace) leading uphill directly behind the bothy. But since I wanted to visit Loch Toll an Lochain in its high corrie under the north-east face of An Teallach, I set off anyway, up steep slopes of deep heather.

Finally, I was able to traverse open screes and scramble down through short crags into the entrance to the legendary corrie, one of the great treasures of the Scottish mountains. There was no menace in it that May morning, the loch lay still and black below the stupendous northern precipices of An Teallach, and the silence was disturbed only by the rattle of an occasional stone coming down the screes. I was quite alone. Patches of snow still hid in the deeper recesses of the gullies, but now, ten days after my first night on the ridge above Loch Arkaig, spring had reached into the mountains and the corrie-walls were green with new growth. Still tired from my long labour the day before, I rested a while by the loch on a platform of smooth sandstone warmed by the sun, then looked for my way down to the Dundonnell road. Skirting the end of the corrie and the base of Glas Meall Mhor, one of the mountain's three great eastern ridges, I soon found traces of a path descending sweeps of polished quartzite in the direction of Coire a' Ghuibhsachain.

*(Top) River and alder
at Achnelgie*

*Strath na Sealga,
at Shenavall*

Strath na Sealga and Shenavall

Coire Toll an Lochain, An Teallach

At first, and for quite a distance down into the lower corrie, the faint traces of the path were emphasized by cairns. Lower, as rock turned to heather and the path became more obvious, the streams of the corrie gathered into one powerful flow, which plummeted in a series of falls and rapids down steepening slopes past lonely pine-trees - outposts of the woods below. The last half-mile to the road was through this sweet-smelling wood of tall and stately pines, whose carpet of needles gave way to a dense undergrowth of glossy rhododendron along the banks of the stream.

I stepped out from this near-jungle on to the road at noon, and crossed it to take the side-road, whose sign-post said Badralloch, over the Dundonnell River and into leafy shade. This pleasant country lane is followed all the way to the start of the Altnaharry track - one of the longest stretches on a paved road on my entire route, but a road with the virtue of being one of the quietest in the Highlands. The first mile is very pleasant, through the broad-leaved woodland around Dundonnell House, and at the solitary cottage at Eilan Darach I turned sharp right to begin a long slow climb, continuous from here to Loch na h'Airbhe three and a half miles away. The road enters a plantation, and after another mile emerges above it on the open hillside where, as more height is gained, a vast moorland plateau can be seen falling gently to the shores of Little Loch Broom. The shapely hill Sail Mhor rises beyond the loch, and looking to the south, An Teallach dominates the landscape, massive and brooding, though not from this perspective, beautiful.

Above the road, steep grass slopes are topped by a line of crags which fall from the summit ridge of Beinn nam Ban. A broad easy gully can be followed up to the ridge, which leads over the top and down to Loch na h'Airbhe. Though this squat and shapeless hill holds little intrinsic interest as a climb, its isolated summit gives a 360-degree panorama which includes the Outer Hebrides, the peaks of Coigach, Assynt and central Sutherland as far north as Ben Klibreck, Ben Dearg, the Fannichs, and An Teallach. On a clear day the view more than repays the effort required to take this high route, and at any time it is a much more rewarding walk than the road. On the first walk I was put off by the prospect of hauling my heavy pack up to the ridge, and decided to stay with the easier of the alternatives, on the road. Where the gradient starts to ease, the metalled road turns sharp left, and the roughest of tracks heads off right. This is the approach to Allt na h'Airbhe - a luxury hotel, reputedly the most expensive in the Highlands. Their guests don't use the pot-holed track, but are ferried across Loch Broom, and by arrangement with the boat-man who works freelance from Ullapool, I was to cross with him on one of his regular trips.

Beyond Loch na h'Airbhe the track began to descend steepening slopes leading sea-wards, with good views north over Loch Broom and Ullapool. Down at the shore, I waited an hour to the unaccustomed sound of breaking waves, brewing tea in the shelter of a rocky cove, and when the boat arrived the short crossing was in pleasant contrast to all the days of foot-slogging. I intended to use Ullapool to stock up on supplies, and get some 'r & r' again. Although it was only two days since I had last slept in a bed, those days had been long and hard, and had seen me cover another twenty-seven miles. My total was now a hundred and fourteen, and I had passed the half-way mark.

Autumn in Dundonnell; An Teallach through the trees

On the Dundonnell road

Little Loch Broom and Sail Mhor

Loch Broom, Ullapool and the north,
from Beinn nam Ban

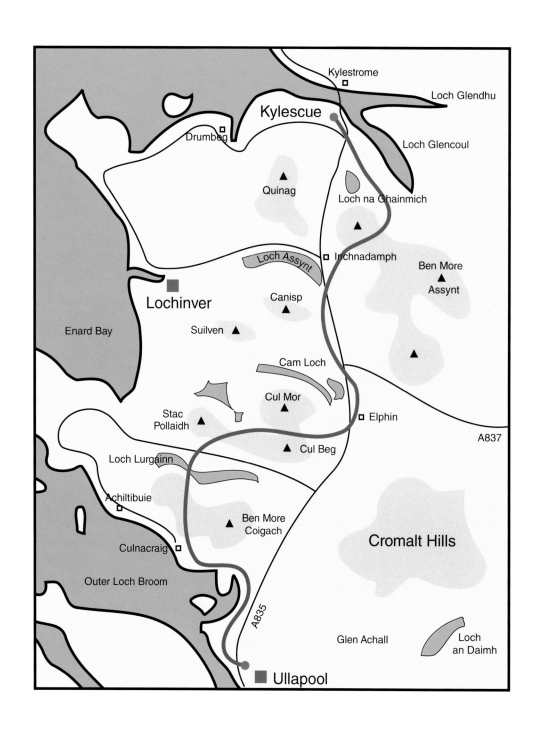

CHAPTER FIVE
ULLAPOOL TO KYLESCUE

1. Ullapool to Culnacraig

Ullapool was originally a 'clearance village' founded in the late eighteenth century by the British Fisheries Society to provide a home and livelihood for crofters turned off their land during the clearances. Today the little port is still home to a large fishing fleet - mainly East European in origin - and it is a common sight to see Loch Broom filled virtually from end to end by trawlers and factory-ships. Though so far I had seen the distant sea twice during the journey, at Strathcarron and Little Loch Broom, my wish to spend some time by it had not been fulfilled until I reached Allt na h'Airbhe on the previous afternoon, to cross Loch Broom by boat to Ullapool. Now, for an entire day, my route lay along the shore.

At Ullapool duckpond

I left the town by the footbridge across the Ullapool River, through the park with its duckpond and out on to the foreshore beyond a muddy estuary. Above the gravelly beach, short springy turf, close-cropped by sheep, made walking pleasant, and progress was rapid. Below Morefield, boats at every possible stage of disintegration lay in a field behind a dry-stone dike, and on the shingle a fishing-boat was beached, high enough to be safe from even spring-tides.

The weather was hot and hazy, the sun had beamed down again all morning from a cloudless sky, and with typical dissatisfaction I was beginning to wish for something different. Had I only known it, this was one wish to be granted all too soon.

Ullapool and Loch Broom

Beached fishing-boat at Morefield

The Lighthouse at Rubha Cadail

Loch Kanaird

Near Rhue, I forded the Allt an t'Strathain and cut uphill to the road which serves this tiny community, following it to where it peters out above grassy slopes which lead down to the small unmanned lighthouse on its rocky promontory at Rubha Cadhail. The light stands looking to Outer Loch Broom, but the waters of the loch were empty of Czech and Polish klondykers as I took to rock and heather slopes which provided an interesting but rather prolonged scramble to bypass short sea-cliffs on the further side of the headland. North, there were fine views across Loch Kanaird, and the sensuous curve of beach at Ardmair, to Ben More Coigach.

I regained the road behind Ardmair Bay, whose off-sized shingle does not make comfortable walking, and stayed on it for a mile to where an unpaved road turns left for Keanchulish House and the River Kanaird. This road winds along the riverbank to a substantial bridge and turns south, and two hundred yards beyond the bridge I struck due west across boggy ground, to pick up the coastal path to Achiltibuie. There is a rapid height-gain on the path almost immediately, and more good views back to Loch Kanaird and the fertile Keanchulish peninsula, with the long and graceful sweep of another beach, Camas Mor, directly below.

From here to Culnacraig was a long and strenuous walk (deceptively short on the map) which was once a postal delivery route to Culnacraig and Achiltibuie. It is hard to imagine walking a return journey along this path, carrying a heavy mail-bag, but it was never difficult to follow, and though it is sketchy in places there are prominent way-markers wherever a mistake might be made. A couple of sections are spectacular, where the path is narrow above tall cliffs falling directly to the water, but these merely add interest to the walk. The high points give stunning views over Isle Martin to Outer Loch Broom and The Minch, and the descents end in bosky hollows served by clear streams which gush down from the hill-slopes above.

Ben More Coigach looms overhead as Culnacraig is approached, and imposes more with every onward step; however, the path is never really close to the sea until directly below the mountain's west ridge, where it is squeezed tightly between crags and foreshore. At the very foot of the ridge, a tiny clearing at

Factory ship in Loch Broom

the base of high, tumbled rocks, floored with moss and bordered by a sparkling stream, tempted me to bivouac, but as usual it was too early in the day to stop. Instead I sat a while, enjoying the calm beauty of the place, and because I had already found the day quite long and hard enough.

There was still a long mile uphill though, to the first house at Culnacraig, and when I reached it my energy had gone. I rested my back against the warm stone wall of an empty holiday cottage for twenty minutes, drinking hot tea and looking out against a hard glare over distant scattered islands; as I did so a sudden wind, cold and penetrating, came sweeping round from the Ben More Coigach ridge behind me. Within what seemed only moments, the temperature had fallen from mild to near-frigid, and I was scrambling in my rucksack for warm clothing not needed since I left Fort William. The wind was rising by the minute, and though I could see that there was shelter of a kind to be had near at hand, I really didn't fancy a bivouac. Instead, at some vague inner prompting, I set off, reluctantly this time, along the road towards Achiltibuie to look for a bed for the night.

2. Achiltibuie to Inchnadamph.

The route northwards from Culnacraig, through the Ben More Coigach *massif* and the hills of south Assynt, probably gives the finest day's walking of the whole trip. Where a stream called the Allt a' Choire Reidh comes down out of the hills, a path leaves the road and climbs up through bracken and heather beside the water. Following the path to where it finally peters out on a bare hillslope, then going straight ahead up this round hump of a hill, brings you in very little time, but not without some pain, to a minor summit of the Coigach range - Beinn nan Caorach - from which the unfolding panorama of islands, sea and sky is unsurpassed in Scotland. Nearby in the south-east, the long serrated crest of Ben More Coigach towers over the intervening slopes of Sgurr an Fhidhleir, and beyond the sharp spike of Carn Conmheall to the west, the long peninsula of Rubha Mhor, dotted with both crofts and innumerable tarns and lochans, reaches far out into The Minch.

The route heads north along a broad ridge, and Beinn nan Caorach dips to a stony col, decorated with wind-sculpted sandstone tors, then rises gently to a second, lower summit.

Outer Loch Broom from Culnacraig

Achiltibuie, and the Assynt and
Coigach Hills, from the west

Loch Lurgainn and Stac Pollaidh

These northern slopes of Beinn Nan Caorach are sheer, and the view is no less than aerial. Spread out below is a paradise of woodland, water, moor and mountain, whose nearer constituents gleam in the clear mountain air, fading by degrees with distance, until the furthest outlines dim into the blue.

Immediately below is Loch Lurgainn of a hundred scalloped bays, and the narrows (which must be crossed) connecting it to Loch Bad na h'Achlaise; above and beyond the loch, the monoliths of Stac Pollaidh, Cul Mor and Cul Beg rise from rolling moorland like monsters from the deep; over their shoulders peer Canisp, Suilven and Quinag; seen through a distant gap Ben More Assynt hides in cloud. Far to the north there are hints of still more distant ridges, and over all this the early sun pours golden light. It is a landscape as if from an earlier age of the world; a view to make your heart beat faster, to make you feel that life is, after all, worth living.

Unfortunately, I saw none of this idealised vision that morning, though on later visits it was almost made real. Instead, as I stepped out into the Achiltibuie morning, dark heavy cloud, illuminated luridly from below, hung around the ridges of the hills and over the sea, and a bitter wind blew strongly from the east. It was as cold as any winter morning, and on all visible hill-slopes down to about five hundred feet above sea-level, snow lay thickly. While I stared around in dismay, snow-flakes whirled down the wind. I stood a minute or two, perplexed, wondering if my walk was over (I wasn't equipped for snow) when a van stopped and I was offered a ride towards Ullapool. There was no time to weigh the pros and cons; I jumped in, and decided to go with them as far as the car-park under Stac Pollaidh. What I most wanted was to continue the walk, but I also needed to test conditions up in the hills, somewhere retreat, if it became necessary, would be short and straightforward. My route from Stac Pollaidh to Cul Mor was on a good track for the first mile or two, and on familiar ground the whole way. Assuming that all went well, I would continue to Elphin, but if conditions were too difficult, or simply too cold for enjoyment, I could easily pull back to the road.

If I had walked my planned route over Beinn nan Caorach and across the Loch Lurgainn narrows, the six or so miles of rough walking would have taken me at least until mid-day; I had gained four hours by accepting the lift, and since further progress on foot might be slow, the time saved was welcome. I walked a mile east along the road to a muddy layby below a stand of stunted pines, and took the path which climbs away from the road though the trees. This is the climbers' track to Cul Mor, and crosses the wide, low pass between Stac Pollaidh and Cul Beg. Wearing every available stitch of clothing, I marched up the well-defined path into the north-east wind, going fast to work up some heat.

At first there was almost no lying snow, but descending the northern slopes into the glen below Cul Mor there was snow behind every clump of grass and heather, and above Loch an Doire Dhuibh the birches thrashed in the rising wind, and gave no shelter. Since there was little point in stopping, for photography or any other reason, I made good time around the head of the loch and down to the river in the valley-bottom where I knew there was a crossing. Snow lay everywhere here, and the wind whistled through the narrow glen between Cul Mor and Cul Beg as I swayed over snow-crusted stepping stones, nervous of a slip into water that looked icy.

My route from here climbs the lower slopes of Cul Mor on to the western terrace of the mountain, and traverses round and into the corrie which separates the main hill-mass from its minor, eastern summit - An Laogh. On the steeper slopes I slipped and stumbled in deepening snow, clutching at heather branches with gloveless hands, and cursing Scottish weather. But most of the scramble to the terrace was accomplished without any real difficulty (and even with enjoyment) though in bitter cold, and having reached the loch which fills the lower half of the corrie I felt happy to continue, as the all main problems were now behind me. Beyond the loch, choppy and streaked with foam, I found what shelter I could among the boulders below An Laogh, to heat water for reviving tea.

The walk to the head of the pass above the loch was longer than it looked, and the wind brought heavy snow-flurries. I plodded up sandy inclines, covered with three inches of wet snow, and pockmarked with the hoof-prints of a herd of deer which skittered past as I sheltered by the loch. Soon, the bluffs either side closed in as the top approached.

*(Top) Lochan Dearg
and An Laogh*

*Loch Lurgainn and
Beinn an Oin*

Canisp, from above the Cam Loch

(Top) The Cam Loch,
with Cul Mor

Un-named lochans north
of Glas Bheinn

Through the An Laogh gap, visibility was poor and I chose the line of least resistance down open slopes towards Elphin; by keeping a small stream on my right I knew I would strike Loch an Laoigh, and beyond that, the Knockan Nature Trail. When the loch finally appeared - a black smear two hundred feet below through driving sleet - I skirted it to the north and carried on to strike the path after another half-mile, following it easily down to the main Ullapool to Ledmore road.

It was only three o'clock. There was a perverse pleasure to be had now in trudging up the road into the blizzard, and before I thought much about it, I had left Elphin behind. An hour later, as I took the left fork at the Ledmore junction, the pleasure was diminishing. There was virtually no traffic on the road, or I might have weakened sooner, but at about five pm I stuck my thumb out at a passing car, and gratefully accepted a lift along the last three miles to Inchnadamph.

3. Inchnadamph to Kylescue.

In spite of the snow, since Ullapool I had walked at least another twenty-nine miles, making my total one hundred and forty-three, not counting car trips. That night I pored over maps, wondering endlessly whether I could have stuck to my intended route, and looking at possibilities for the next day, should the weather stay poor.

My planned line to Kylescue takes the estate path north-east up the glen behind the hotel at Inchnadamph, swings past Loch Fleodach Coire and continues to the pass behind Glas Bheinn. Beyond a pair of un-named lochans it traverses under Cnoc a Creige and follows the east shore of Loch na Ghainmich, at whose northern end a waterfall plunges dramatically into a narrow limestone gorge. The route continues past the falls and climbs to the top of Cnoc Coire a'Bhaic, dropping down its terminal ridge to finish by road to Kylescue. This is all superb walking country, with unusual views of the rugged wilderness of central Sutherland, finishing in the shadow of Quinag, along the shores of Loch Glencoul.

With the snow lying deeper on the hills than ever, this route was too demanding, and I decided to take the obvious option of following the shores of Loch Assynt to Skiag Bridge, then the road to Kylescue. The last mile was briefly illuminated by a rare glimpse of sun.

Ben More Assynt from Inchnadamph

Quinag from the east

Loch Glencoul

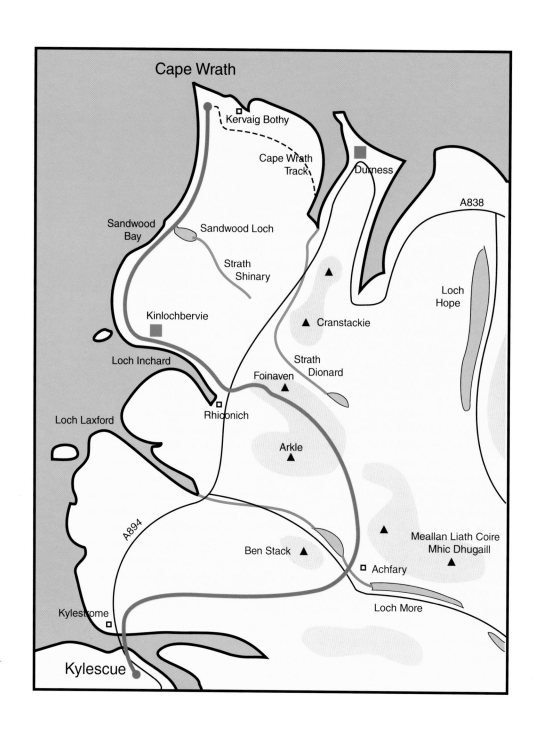

Chapter Six
Kylescue To Cape Wrath

1. Kylescue to Achfary

From Kylescue, I crossed the new bridge over the mouth of Loch Glendhu, and beyond Kylestrome took the private road which goes off right at the end of a small belt of conifers. East of the trees the road goes only as far as a couple of small estate cottages, and becomes a well-engineered footpath, drained and ballasted, which climbs above the north shores of Loch Glendhu to make a high cross-country traverse to Achfary in Glenmore. It was here, on a later visit, that I had a slightly unusual encounter with a red-deer stag.

Loch Glendhu

It was late in the season, and I thought the rut well past, making me safe from both estate shooting parties and irritable stags; not a half-a-mile beyond the cottages I came on a group of stags lying together on a grassy hillside, confirming that the rut really was over. We were separated by a fence, and beyond it a young single-point stag stood alone, eyeing me coldly; he began to trot towards the fence, and in a moment had cleared it; as he lowered his head and picked up speed, I realised my first thought - that the estate might be putting out feed for the deer, and this stag had mistaken me for a keeper - was misplaced! There was no point in trying to run from a stag; the path was stony and I picked up a couple of big ones; as soon as he was in range I let fly. The first just glanced off his flank, but he shied and raised his head; with the second I caught him full on the chest and stopped him. He was unhappy about giving up, though, and stood barking and waving his antlers at me until I picked up another couple of stones. At this he turned and trotted off towards the herd, which had been disturbed by our jousting and was making off round the hill to the north. When they were all well out of sight and my heart had stopped pounding I continued on my eastern path, casting a wary eye from time to time on the direction they had taken.

Some months later there was a sequel, when I met up with one of the local keepers, and told him the story. He was highly amused, and recognised my descriptions of both the stag and its behaviour, neither of which were unknown to him. The animal was an out-and-out renegade and had already chased a couple of estate workers; it was also given to running up to anyone out on the track in a Landrover and baring its teeth at them! The keepers had their collective eye on him, however, and this young stag would be unlikely to survive the winter cull. I never checked whether they did manage to shoot him, but I never saw him again, either.

From the track, there are broad views south and east, and though the snow had relented the wind was strong, and the sky grey and stormy again. Evening was approaching and I hurried on, marking my progress by the numerous small lochans at the track-side, stopping only once to make a hot drink in the lee of a fine stone-built bridge which took the footpath over a large stream. Beyond the ruins of a solitary sheiling I dropped down towards Achfary, into the welcome shelter of a dark and dense plantation.

2. Achfary to Rhiconich.

Cape Wrath was near now, and my walk was nearing a conclusion. Looking at a map of the area, the most logical walking route from Achfary goes by the un-metalled road to Lone on the south-east corner of Loch Stack, and continues up the valley of the River Horn behind Arkle and Foinaven. Below the broad southern slopes of Foinaven it crosses an un-named sixteen-hundred-foot pass and drops down into the cleft of upper Strath Dionard. This long, deep valley and its less dramatic continuation, Strath Shinary, lead directly north-west to the coast at Sandwood Bay, just seven or eight miles south of Cape Wrath.

Ruined sheiling above Achfary

Woods at Achfary

The bothy at Lone

(Top) Glen More and Arkle

Cranstackie from Foinaven

I left Achfary on another morning of biting east winds intending to finish the walk in two more days, bivouacking somewhere in Glen Shinary. The level track to the locked bothy at Lone passed quickly, but the cold was so severe that I took shelter for a while in a stand of conifers which huddle under the tail of Arkle's long south ridge. The Allt Horn runs through the trees in a shallow ravine which deepens upstream to where a fine waterfall, difficult to see, drops over a sheer cliff. I regained the path above the trees and followed it round the north side of the narrow winding glen of the Allt Horn, and under the rocks of Creagan Meall Horn, to the start of the descent into Strath Dionard. At the pass, Ben Hope glowered in the east below a layer of dark cloud, snow-filled gullies seaming its black cliffs. Nearer at hand, the wild cirque of naked rock behind Meall Horn held two lochans cupped one above the other on narrow terraces; below them, steep slopes pocked with snow fell away towards Strath Dionard, still unseen round a corner of the crags. In these conditions the scene had a primordial quality, intense and untamed, and I felt lonelier and more exposed than I had at any other point on the walk.

In Strath Dionard, after I first descended into the head of the glen, there were a couple of trackless miles to the loch and along its western shore, which gave me perhaps the roughest walking of the entire trip. At the northern end of the loch, where the River Dionard leaves it, an ugly road of imported red soil cuts through the native rock and heather like a scar, stretching all the way to where the Durness road separates Strath Dionard from Strath Shinary. This outrage perpetrated on a previously unspoilt glen was infuriating, and as soon as I could, I sat down with the relevant map to look for a possible change of route. For the time being I contented myself by climbing out of Strath Dionard to the west, over slopes of deep heather, and crossing the wide stretch of moorland below the north ridge of Foinaven.

I hit the road near the point marked Clach a'Bhoinead on the map, and walked two miles west along the road to the friendly hotel at the Rhiconich junction, not sorry to be able to enjoy a night's warmth and comfort again (in another of my favourite hotels) instead of a cold bivouac on the shores of Loch Shinary.

Western panorama from the summit of Foinaven

Ben Stack from Rhiconich

3. Rhiconich to Cape Wrath.

Since leaving Inchnadamph I reckoned to have covered around thirty-three miles, and Cape Wrath was, at most, only a day and a half's walk away. Study of maps that night at Rhiconich and since, and some testing of alternatives on the ground, has led me to a route from Achfary which still follows the Foinaven track past the bothy at Lone and up to the col above Strath Dionard, but then climbs Foinaven (you are halfway up anyway), and continues along its main ridge (there are no difficulties). From the northern summit it descends northwest to the road - striking it very much where I had - and continues down to Rhiconich. Any walker who has reached Achfary will be very fit and able to tackle the climb, and it seems appropriate to celebrate approaching success on the walk by climbing its most northerly mountain, with its fine vistas of the Sutherland hills and the tundra stretching away towards Cape Wrath.

From Rhiconich there is only one possible continuation - through Kinlochbervie and the other townships along the Loch Inchard road, reaching Sandwood Bay by the path from Balchrick, and on across the moors to Cape Wrath. Leaving Rhiconich, it was interesting, for once, to have houses and crofts to look at; fishing-boats in Kinlochbervie harbour; the foundations of a new school, and even a few people around. I turned on to the Sandwood track at eleven am, and was on the sands by one. It was utterly deserted, with not a footprint except my own, but on a grey day of frequent rain showers (the freeze had gone) the legendary beauty of the place was hardly at its best and there was nothing to keep me long. Though Sandwood Bay was a place I had already visited many times, on a better afternoon I should certainly have stayed to explore the beach again - and the remarkable lagoon behind it - finding, in some sheltered corner of the dunes, a place to sleep. But that would have to be another time; a chill east wind discouraged any desire to linger, and after a look at the surf, I kept moving.

At the north end of the beach, boots and socks had to come off for the crossing of the river which flows out of Sandwood Loch, not half a mile away behind the sand-dunes. After quite some hesitation I stepped in, and on the far bank moments later had to laugh at my own cowardice. It was icy cold, though.

Loch Inchard at Rhiconich

Net floats, Kinlochbervie

(Opp) Sandwood Bay

The lagoon at Sandwood

Cape Wrath

During the walk up the track to Sandwood, a bank of fog had been advancing slowly from the east. It crept remorselessly on, and as I climbed the grassy bank at the end of the beach I saw that it must soon envelope me. I kept on a steady course along the cliff-top, leaving the edge a hundred yards or so to my left, and soon the fog swept silently over, deadening all sound, and quickly becoming dense enough to have me make occasional checks with map and compass.

Several streams crossed my path, heading for the sea, and I counted these off against the map; one of them, the Keisgaig River, was a fair-sized stream. The fog was very thick now, and I was glad to recognise, above the Keisgaig, the truly miniature col between two hillocks which rejoice in the names Sithean na h'Iolaireth and Cnoc a'Ghuibhais. As I came through between them, there was a shifting in the air, and for a moment the mist thinned. Straight ahead, perhaps a mile away, a small circular loch was cupped on the summit of another hill, and now my bearings were complete. I followed a tributary trickle downhill and found a neat little valley, as symmetrical as a railway cutting, which

swung away to the north-east. I had just dropped down into this, to follow it towards the Cape Wrath track, when the foghorn began. There was no need for any further navigation, and all that I had to do was follow the sound, distant and muted at first, but growing steadily louder as I approached, until it was almost painful. A few minutes later I passed through open gates into the grounds of the lighthouse, still invisible in the fog.

It was five-thirty pm on my seventeenth day since leaving Banavie, all those long miles away, and the walk was complete. The fog-horn boomed out to the four winds as if announcing my arrival, vapour swirled in the restless cliff-top air and the white-painted buildings shouldered the mist aside one moment and receded back into it like ghosts the next. I stood silently for a minute or two to savour it all, running back in my mind through the days and miles south to where I started out along the Caledonian Canal, then headed for where there was light in a window.

Towards evening the fog slowly cleared and later the sun gleamed briefly out through a band of dark clouds along the horizon.

The following day was gloriously fine.

Cape Wrath and the lighthouse

Epilogue
Home, And Other Directions

Cape Wrath is far from any public road, and this could be seen as a problem! There is transport, however. During the summer months - roughly from May to September - a minibus plies the fifteen miles of rough track between the Cape and the Kyle of Durness, a shallow fjord penetrating deep inland from the north coast. A boatman waits to ferry you across, and from there it's up to you - hitch to Durness for a postbus to Thurso, or to Lairg for a train south; the warm glow of success will sustain you on the journey! I was lucky enough to be picked up, and after a day's rest set off again, to collect my car and head for home. In all the months which followed, my head was full of the walk, and I was often back in the north, working on the collection of photographs, and on the line of the walk itself. I traversed the Foinaven ridge and found it to be much more enjoyable than Strath Dionard. There are other possible routes here, including a line between Arkle and Foinaven, an exciting cross-country route between Inchnadamph and Achfary, and other variations further south in Torridon - some of which I have tried, and others which are still just lines on a map.

I hope to do it all again one day, in the right company, and it would be wonderful to start in Glasgow and walk all the way to Cape Wrath on a properly recognised trail. But maybe this is hoping for too much. Come what may, the route will always be there now, for any who might want to walk the glorious hills and glens of the walk I've dared to call - The Cape Wrath Trail.

The Kyle of Durness